PAMELA .I. EMMANUEL

MONARCH

WOMAN KING ARISE

MONARCH

Woman King Arise

MONARCH

Table Of Contents

Woman King Arise

MONARCH

MONARCH

MONARCH

MONARCH

MONARCH

MONARCH

Woman King Arise

MONARCH

Meet the Author: Pamela I. Emmanuel

Embracing My Royal Identity: A Journey from Trials to Triumph

Introduction

From the earliest days of my life, God's hand was unmistakably upon me. Born into a family steeped in faith and fervent prayer, my upbringing was a unique blend of challenges and divine preparation. Growing up in a predominantly Caucasian community as part of one of the few African American families, I quickly learned the art of resilience. My Nigerian heritage, rich with culture and tradition, was a source of strength, yet my strict upbringing also made me stand out in a world that often felt foreign. Even as a child, I was drawn to the supernatural, miracles, signs wonders and spiritual warfare that surrounded me, unaware that the battles I waged in prayer then were preparing me for the greater battles I would face as an adult.

I remember those early days vividly—the sense of being different, the longing for acceptance, and the subtle yet persistent feeling that I was being forged for something greater.

9 - 117

MONARCH

My parents, deeply rooted in the Christian faith, instilled in me the importance of prayer, the power of scripture, and the necessity of spiritual warfare. What I didn't realize at the time was that these lessons were laying the foundation for my future —a future that would be marked by both extraordinary victories and devastating setbacks.

The Cost of Being Chosen

In the journey of faith, being chosen by God is both an honor and a heavy responsibility. It means you are set apart for a mighty work, yet it also means you are a prime target for the enemy. To be chosen is to be marked for greatness, but it also means enduring trials, opposition, and the weight of the calling. The lives of biblical figures who were chosen by God resonate deeply with my own experiences. Being chosen has often meant walking a path of rejection, pain, and spiritual warfare.

Take, for example, Joseph. He was chosen to save a nation (Genesis 37-50). Favored by his father, but despised by his brothers, Joseph was sold into slavery, falsely accused, and imprisoned. Yet, through these trials, he remained faithful, and God used him to save Egypt and his own family from famine. Joseph's story is a powerful reminder that being chosen often involves betrayal and suffering.

MONARCH

Like Joseph, I have experienced betrayal, lies, false accusation and character assassination, but I have also seen how God can turn these trials into triumphs.

Moses was another chosen one, tasked with leading the Israelites out of Egypt (Exodus 2-4). He faced immense opposition from Pharaoh and even his own people. He endured rejection and frustration, often feeling inadequate for the task. Moses' journey resonates with my own struggles of feeling rejected and inadequate. Growing up in a predominantly Caucasian neighborhood as the only Nigerian family, I faced rejection because of my race, my physique, and my family's conservative values. Like Moses, I have learned that being chosen often means standing out and enduring the pain of not fitting in.

David, too, was chosen to be king (1 Samuel 16-30). Anointed while still a young shepherd, David's path to the throne was filled with danger and betrayal. He was hunted by King Saul, lived as a fugitive, and faced numerous battles. David's story mirrors my own experiences with "church leaders" and mentors who were envious and practiced covetous witchcraft & occult practices against me. Being chosen often means being targeted by those who feel threatened by your calling. Even Esther, chosen to save her people, faced the cost of her calling (Esther 4:14). As queen, her position came with great risk.

MONARCH

The reality is that being chosen by God comes with a price, and I have paid it in many ways, including through the trials of marriage, divorce, smear campaigns and relentless spiritual warfare.

The Dream That Turned Into a Nightmare

Fast forward to a decade ago, and it seemed like I was living a dream. I was a "happily" married woman, celebrating a quarter-million-dollar dream wedding at the magnificent Parisian Chateau (Cocomar) Nouvelle in Houston, Texas.

The event was nothing short of spectacular—250 guests from around the world, a stunning multilayered cake adorned with 24-karat gold (my favorite color), and a beautiful white Mercedes Benz as a wedding gift. My husband was an Ivy League graduate and an international businessman of Igbo heritage, with a luxurious penthouse in Beverly Hills. To the outside world, I had it all. But appearances can be deceiving. Despite the trappings of success and the fairy tale wedding, my marriage was far from perfect. In fact, it was a crucible that tested my faith, my identity, and my resilience. I became the first in my family to get divorced and become a single mother, a reality that brought unbearable shame, pain, and inner turmoil.

MONARCH

The questions were relentless: How could I have made such a monumental mistake? How did I end up here, despite knowing better? The shame was so intense that I couldn't face my hometown, so I relocated to Los Angeles, seeking a fresh start and a place to heal.

In the midst of this dark season, when all seemed lost, I cried out to the Lord. It was in that moment of utter brokenness that I heard His resounding voice, declaring one word that would change the trajectory of my life: **REIGN!**

From Ashes to Beauty: The Call to Reign

God's declaration over my life in that moment was not just a word; it was a commissioning—a divine mandate to rise, rule, and reign as a Monarch Woman King. Isaiah 61:3 (NIV) became a lifeline for me: "To bestow on them a crown of beauty instead of ashes, the oil of joy instead of mourning, and a garment of praise instead of a spirit of despair." I realized that my trials, as painful as they were, were not the end of my story. They were, in fact, the very fires that were refining me for the greater purpose God had ordained for me. Behold, I have refined thee, but not with silver; I have tested you in the furnace of affliction. Isaiah 48:10

13 - 117

MONARCH

As I began to embrace my sovereign identity, I understood that my past did not define me. Rather, it was the platform from which God would launch me into my destiny. Psalm 139:16 (NIV) reminded me, "Your eyes saw my unformed body; all the days ordained for me were written in your book before one of them came to be." God had written my story long before I ever walked through these trials, and His plans for me were for good, not for harm (Jeremiah 29:11, NIV).

Encouragement to You, My Reader

Where are you today? Have you made mistakes? Do you feel lost, ashamed, or confused? I want to encourage you with this truth: We all make mistakes, but those mistakes do not have to define your future. Romans 8:28 (NIV) assures us, "And we know that in all things God works for the good of those who love him, who have been called according to his purpose." You have a loving Father in heaven who has written a book about you, decreeing His plans over your life. Rise, pick up your bed, and walk (John 5:8, NIV). He's not mad at you; turn to Him, repent, get back up, and get back on track. If you're struggling, I encourage you to seek Him with all your heart. James 4:8 (NIV) promises, "Come near to God and he will come near to you." Remember, He makes everything beautiful in His time (Ecclesiastes 3:11, NIV). This is not your end; it's merely the beginning of a new chapter in your life.

Woman King Arise

MONARCH

Conclusion

As I continue to walk in my calling, I am ever reminded of the power of God's grace, the strength found in His Word, and the authority that comes from embracing our identity in Christ. My journey has been marked by trials, yes, but also by triumphs that can only be attributed to His unfailing love and mercy. And this same grace, this same power, is available to you.

Welcome to Monarch Woman King Arise, where I unveil the profound wisdom gleaned from my journey, shared with raw honesty and divine insight. In a world craving genuine inspiration, my prayer is that the revelations within these pages will empower you to rise with unshakable strength, embrace your royal heritage with bold courage, and step into your destiny as a sovereign heir of the Kingdom of God. May you be invigorated by the Kingdom authority bestowed upon you and ignited to reign with the grace and power that is your birthright.

15 – 117

MONARCH

Introduction

Understanding the Kingdom of Heaven and Kingdom of God

The message of the Kingdom of Heaven/God is at the heart of Jesus Christ's teachings and the entirety of Scripture. While "Kingdom of Heaven" and "Kingdom of God" are often used interchangeably, they each have distinct focuses and implications. Grasping their nuances is essential for fully understanding what it means to live as a King and Priest unto God, walking in the Kingdom authority and Dominion bestowed upon us by our Divine Sovereign.

The Kingdom of Heaven

The Kingdom of Heaven represents the territorial domain governed by God's sovereign authority—a realm where His will is perfectly executed, and His sovereignty remains unchallenged. Unlike the kingdoms of this world, the Kingdom of Heaven operates according to divine principles, as vividly illustrated through various parables by Jesus. Jesus frequently used parables to convey the nature and values of the Kingdom of Heaven, beginning many teachings with, "The Kingdom of Heaven is like..." These parables reveal how the Kingdom contrasts with worldly realms and highlight its transformative and expansive nature.

MONARCH

For example, the Mustard Seed parable (Matthew 13:31-32) likens the Kingdom to a mustard seed—small and insignificant at first, yet growing into something grand and impactful. This illustrates how the Kingdom starts from humble beginnings but grows to exert significant influence.

Similarly, the **Hidden Treasure** parable (Matthew 13:44) describes the Kingdom as a treasure hidden in a field, emphasizing its immense value and the total commitment required to obtain it. The **Pearl of Great Price** (Matthew 13:45-46) further underscores this point by comparing the Kingdom to a precious pearl, which a merchant sells everything to acquire, illustrating the supreme value of the Kingdom.

In the **Dragnet** parable (Matthew 13:47-50), the Kingdom is depicted as a net that gathers all kinds of fish, symbolizing the final separation of the righteous from the wicked. The **Wedding Feast** parable (Matthew 22:2-14) portrays the Kingdom as a royal banquet where initial invitees reject the invitation, leading to an inclusive call to everyone, but also stressing the need for proper preparation and righteousness.

MONARCH

The **Ten Virgins** parable (Matthew 25:1-13) illustrates the Kingdom as a wedding where preparedness is crucial, highlighting that only those ready for the bridegroom's arrival are admitted.

Finally, the **Talents** parable (Matthew 25:14-30) compares the Kingdom to a master's investment in his servants, emphasizing the importance of faithful stewardship and the rewards for those who effectively use their gifts.

These parables collectively convey that the Kingdom of Heaven, though starting from modest beginnings, grows into something profound and valuable. They also teach that true participation in the Kingdom requires commitment, readiness, and responsible stewardship.

The Kingdom of God (on Earth), on the other hand, refers to the territory called Earth, owned by the Creator of all, but still to be conformed to the law, authority and dominion of the Creator. This is God's reign and rule in the hearts and lives of believers and within the world. A present spiritual reality that is manifested on Earth wherever God's authority is recognized and obeyed.

MONARCH

The Kingdom of God is within us (Luke 17:21), indicating that when we submit to God's authority and allow Him to govern us and demonstrate through our lives, we become an active participant of His Kingdom. This Kingdom is marked by righteousness, peace, and joy in the Holy Spirit (Romans 14:17). It is a dynamic force that impacts every area of our lives and has the power to change the world. As believers, we are called to seek first the Kingdom of God and His righteousness, trusting that all other things will be added to us (Matthew 6:33).

- **The Kingdom of God is righteousness, peace, and joy in the Holy Spirit (Romans 14:17)** The Kingdom of God is characterized by the transformative work of the Holy Spirit in our lives. It is not merely about external observance of religious rituals but about the internal realities of righteousness, peace, and joy that come from a life surrendered to God. The Kingdom of God is experienced within us, changing our inner world and influencing how we live in the external world.

- **The Kingdom of God is not in word but in power (1 Corinthians 4:20)** The Kingdom of God is demonstrated through the power of God working in and through us.

19 – 117

- It is more than just talking about God's rule; it is about living in a way that reflects His authority and power. The Kingdom of God is manifest when we operate in the authority given to us by Christ, overcoming darkness, engage in miracles, signs & wonders, and advancing God's purposes on Earth.

- **The Kingdom of God is at hand (Mark 1:15)** When Jesus proclaimed that the Kingdom of God is at hand, He was announcing the arrival of God's ruling government in Heaven has now arrived to colonize Earth. This declaration invites us to step into the reality of God's Kingdom now, living in a way that aligns with His will and purpose. The Kingdom of God is a present reality, accessible to us here and now, as we choose to live under God's rule.

The Gospel of the Kingdom

Jesus came not just to preach salvation but to proclaim the Gospel of the Kingdom. His mission was to declare the good news that God's Kingdom had come to earth, and with it, the opportunity for humanity to be restored to right relationship with God. The Gospel of the Kingdom encompasses salvation, deliverance, healing, and the authority to live victoriously as representatives of God's Kingdom on earth.

20 - 117

This Kingdom mandate is rooted in God's original command to humanity: "Be fruitful and multiply, fill the earth and subdue it; have dominion" (Genesis 1:26-28). We are called to extend the influence of God's Kingdom in every sphere of life, taking territory and advancing His purposes on earth. The Divine Promise, the covenant of God to redeem and restore the Kingdom to Earth.

Colonization of the Kingdom

Colonization as we know it is the extension of a kingdom's influence to distant territory. In exploring the concept of the Kingdom of Heaven's colonization of Earth, it becomes evident that this divine initiative transcends mere geographic or political boundaries. Dr. Myles Munroe, a visionary thinker whose teachings remain influential even after his passing, said "the essence of this colonization lies in the establishment of Heaven's values, principles, and governance on Earth". Just as a sovereign kingdom extends its influence to new territories, the Kingdom of Heaven seeks to manifest its spiritual dominion through the lives of its citizens.

This divine mandate is not about physical conquest but about transforming human lives and societies according to the righteous standards and eternal wisdom of Heaven.

MONARCH

The colonization of Earth by the Kingdom of Heaven involves a profound reorientation of human thought, behavior, and societal structures, aligning them with the principles of justice, peace, and love that define the heavenly realm. In this divine strategy, the role of believers is crucial—they are not merely passive recipients but active agents who embody and propagate the values of the Kingdom, heralding a new era of spiritual awakening and transformation.

The seventh angel sounded his trumpet, and there were loud voices in heaven, which said: 'The kingdom of the world has become the kingdom of our Lord and of his Messiah, and he will reign for ever and ever.'" Revelation 11:15, as the prophetic vision foretells. This transformation signifies more than a shift in political power; it represents a profound reordering of the entire fabric of human existence.

As the Kingdom of Heaven extends its reach, it brings with it a new paradigm of governance, justice, and righteousness that transcends earthly systems. The colonization of Earth by Heaven's Kingdom is a divine reclamation of human culture and society, infusing them with heavenly values and principles. It is a process of renewing and restoring every sphere of life—be it personal, communal, or institutional—so that they reflect the order, peace, and love that characterize the divine reign.

Woman King Arise

This transition is both a promise and a challenge: a promise of a world transformed by the sovereign will of God, and a challenge to each believer to be an active participant in this divine plan, heralding the coming of a Kingdom that will ultimately unify all creation under the rule of Christ.

Our Sovereign Identity in King Jesus

As we delve into the revelation in Monarch, Woman King arise of the Kingdom of God and the Kingdom of Heaven, this purpose is to help us to recognize that we are not merely observers of the Kingdom—but heirs and active participants. We are called to embody the Kingdom, to live out its principles in our daily lives. As sons of the King, we are also co-heirs with Christ, destined to reign with Him (Romans 8:17). This royal identity is about our birthright, spiritual authority and responsibility. Imagine the transformative power of realizing and actively engaging as a son of the King, destined to reign with Him (Revelation 5:10).

As you delve into these pages, you will uncover the weight of your calling and the splendor of your inheritance. You will learn to wield the scepter of righteousness and wear the crown of glory, for you are chosen, royal, and called for such a time as this (1 Peter 2:9, Esther 4:14).

23 – 117

The Adamic Dominion Mandate

The mandate given to Adam and his seed in Genesis to govern Earth. The Dominion Mandate reflects God's desire for His Kingdom to be established on earth as it is in Heaven. This involves exercising dominion, not through coercion or manipulation, but through righteous leadership, stewardship, and service. We are called to bring the culture of Heaven to earth, influencing every area of society with the values and principles of God's Kingdom.

We are not left to do this on our own in our own human strength. As Kingdom citizens, we have been endowed with authority to carry out this mandate. This authority is not just about power, but about rightful dominion under God's rule.

It involves taking spiritual territory, advancing the Kingdom through prayer, evangelism, and righteous living. It is a call to arise and reign as Kings and Priests in God's Kingdom, enforcing His will on earth.

The Royal Army of God

24 - 117

MONARCH

In this spiritual battle to advance the Kingdom of Heaven in Earth, we are not left defenseless. God has established His royal army, both in Heaven and on Earth, to enforce the victory our King Jesus secured for us against the forces of darkness that seek to oppose His Kingdom. The royal army in Heaven consists of angels who are sent to minister to those who will inherit salvation (Hebrews 1:14). On earth, the royal army includes believers who are equipped with the spiritual armor described in Ephesians 6:10-18. This armor includes the belt of truth, the breastplate of righteousness, the gospel of peace, the shield of faith, the helmet of salvation, and the sword of the Spirit, which is the Word of God. Through prayer, fasting, and spiritual warfare, we are empowered to stand firm against the enemy's schemes, knowing that victory is already secured through Christ.

Conclusion

The Kingdom of Heaven and the Kingdom of God are profound realities that demand our understanding and engagement. As we explore these concepts throughout this book, we will uncover the depth of our identity and authority in Christ, and how we are called to advance His Kingdom on earth. This is not just a call to personal salvation but to a life of purpose, power, and dominion as we embrace our royal identity and fulfill the Kingdom mandate.

Chapter 1: Royal Identity: Kings and Priests Unto God

In the beginning, when God created mankind, He bestowed upon them an identity that was rooted in His own image and likeness. Genesis 1:26-28 records God's declaration: "Let Us make man in Our image, according to Our likeness; let them have dominion..." This was not a casual statement but a profound decree that defined humanity's purpose and identity from the very beginning. We were created to be kings and priests unto God, entrusted with the authority to rule and reign on earth as representatives of His Kingdom.

The Image and Likeness of God

To be made in the image and likeness of God means that we were designed to reflect His nature, character, and authority. This is not merely about physical appearance but about carrying the essence of who God is. As His image-bearers, we are called to mirror His righteousness, holiness, and love in our interactions with the world. We are also endowed with His authority, giving us the ability to govern and steward the earth according to His will. **"The Heaven, even the Heavens, are the Lord's; but the Earth He has given to the children of men."** Psalm 115:16 (NKJV).

26 – 117

MONARCH

This verse emphasizes that while the heavens belong to God, He has entrusted the earth to humanity to steward and govern. It reflects the authority and responsibility given to mankind to rule and manage the earth under God's divine guidance.

The concept of kingship is deeply embedded in this identity. A king is one who has been given authority to rule over a territory, to establish order, and to execute justice. In the spiritual sense, we are called to rule over the realms of our lives—our thoughts, actions, relationships, and the environments in which we live and work. This kingship is not about exercising domination over people but about righteous leadership, serving others while upholding the principles of God's Kingdom.

The Priesthood of Believers

In addition to our kingship, we are also called to be priests unto God. The role of a priest is to mediate between God and man, to offer sacrifices, and to minister in the presence of God. In the Old Testament, the priesthood was reserved for the tribe of Levi, but through Christ, every believer has been made a priest, with direct access to God's presence and the privilege of offering spiritual sacrifices (1 Peter 2:5). This priestly role is integral to our Kingdom identity. As priests, we are called to intercede on behalf of others, to stand in the gap through prayer, and to be ministers of reconciliation.

We carry the responsibility of bringing others into the knowledge of God, leading them into His presence, and facilitating their relationship with Him.

The Reign of Kings and Priests

The combination of kingship and priesthood in our identity is significant. It means that we are not only rulers but also ministers, called to govern with authority and to serve with humility. This dual role reflects the nature of Jesus Christ, who is both King of kings and our Great High Priest. He demonstrated that true leadership is characterized by service, and true authority is exercised in submission to God's will. Our kingship empowers us to take dominion, to subdue the works of darkness, and to advance the Kingdom of God on earth. Our priesthood equips us to stand in the presence of God, to offer prayers and intercession, and to minister His grace and truth to the world. Together, these roles enable us to fulfill our Kingdom mandate, to bring Heaven's influence into every sphere of life. The greatness of a king is directly tied to our role as priests; the strength of our rule is reflected in the sacrifices we make before God. As both king and priest, our leadership is intertwined with our devotion, fulfilling His divine purpose. A king's strength is directly linked to their devotion and effectiveness in priestly functions. One cannot truly reign in power without first excelling in their role as a priest, for it is through the priesthood that divine authority and wisdom flow, enabling righteous and effective rule.

28 – 117

Chapter 2: The New Kingdom Era—A Time of Unveiling and Authority

We are witnessing a monumental Clash of Eras as we transition into the Kingdom Era—the Age of the Kingdom of God. Clashing is never comfortable; it signifies conflict, resistance, or disagreement between people, ideas, or even spiritual forces. In this season, opposing forces collide, and the world is being shaken to its core. Yet, as Kingdom citizens, it's crucial that we remain flexible in God's hands, ready to pivot as He directs. Though everything is being shaken, we are called to stand firm, filled with courage, for Christ has already overcome the world. We know how the story ends: "The kingdoms of this world have become the kingdoms of our Lord and of His Christ, and He shall reign forever and ever!" (Revelation 11:15). "For the earnest expectation of the creation eagerly waits for the revealing of the heirs, sons of God." (Romans 8:19)." In this new Kingdom era, there is a clarion call for the heirs of God to arise and take their rightful place as kings and priests unto God. The enemy has long sought to strip us of our authority, to deceive us into believing that we are powerless and insignificant. This book, "Monarch Woman King Arise," is a call to action. It is a summons for women and men alike to step into their royal identity, to embrace the authority that has been bestowed upon them by God, and to reign as kings and priests in the Kingdom of God.

Woman King Arise

It is a call to reject the deception of the enemy, to reclaim what has been stolen, and to enforce the reign of Christ in every area of life.

We are living in a pivotal time in history—a new era of the Kingdom of God is being unveiled. The old structures are giving way to a fresh move of the Holy Spirit, and there is a divine urgency for the Body of Christ to awaken to its true identity and authority. This is not just a time of transition; it is a time of transformation. The Lord is calling His people to rise up, to step into the fullness of their Kingdom authority, and to reign as He intended from the beginning.

The journey of arising and reigning is not without challenges. There will be battles to fight, mountains to conquer, and opposition to overcome. But we are not alone in this journey. We have been equipped with the armor of God, empowered by the Holy Spirit, surrounded by a great cloud of witnesses who have gone before us.

Our defensive and offensive advantage is the Lion of the Tribe of Judah and the military of the Kingdom of Heaven. As we arise and step into position, we will see the Kingdom of Heaven advance in power and authority, and we will fulfill our divine mandate to rule and reign with Christ and advance His Kingdom.

The Shift from the Spirit of Religion t

30 - 117

Woman King Arise

MONARCH

For too long, many in the Church have been content with religious rituals and traditions, often mistaking them for true spirituality. While religion seeks to bind people to a set of rules and regulations, the Kingdom is about relationship, authority, and dominion. Jesus did not come to establish a religion; He came to establish the Kingdom of God on earth.

In Matthew 6:33, Jesus said, "But seek first the Kingdom of God and His righteousness, and all these things shall be added to you." The Kingdom is not about observing religious customs; it is about seeking and establishing God's rule and reign and becoming a kingdom of royal priests in the Earth.

Extending His influence and the culture of Heaven to colonize in the Earth allowing this be on display for all the world to witness. We do this by aligning ourselves with the Kingdom of Heavens principles, laws, morals, values, culture, customs, constitution, language, ethics and ideals.

The Church is now entering a time where God is stripping away the old religious structures that have hindered the flow of His Spirit and the reign of the government of Heaven.

31 – 117

MONARCH

This is a time of unlearning, where the Holy Spirit is teaching us to operate in Kingdom authority rather than in religious rituals and customs that over emphasize power without authority.

The difference is significant: while power can be exercised by anyone including the devil, authority is granted by God and is rooted in submission to His rulership. Kingdom authority with Kingdom power is essential in this new era.

The Importance of Kingdom Authority with Power

One of the key revelations in this new Kingdom era is that authority is more important than power. Authority comes from God and is bestowed upon those who submit to His rule. In Luke 9:1, we see that Jesus gave His disciples both power and authority over all demons and to cure diseases. This authority was not something they took upon themselves; it was granted by Jesus because they were under His authority. This is why the Lord says, "I have given you authority over all the power of the enemy." While power is often discussed, authority is less frequently addressed. Authority is the permission granted by Jesus to exercise power—the legal right to use it. And Jesus came and spoke to them, saying, "All authority has been given to Me in heaven and on Earth Matt. 28:18.

This distinction is crucial because the kingdom of darkness also wields power. Many occultists, witches, and followers of satan fast, they know the word of God and pray to gain spiritual power. What sets us apart is our God-given authority.

Operating in Kingdom authority requires understanding and acknowledging the source of that authority—Jesus Christ. It is only when we are submitted to His rulership that we can exercise true authority over the spiritual and natural realms. The enemy may have power, but he does not have legitimate authority.

He usurps authority from the sons of God, an example of this is illustrated in the bible when the devil deceived Eve. His power is illegitimate because it is exercised outside of God's order.

In this new era, the Lord is raising up believers who understand their Kingdom authority and who will not be intimidated by the enemy's power. These are those who will recover their usurped authority and will establish the rule and reign of Christ in their spheres of influence, and who will advance the Kingdom with boldness and authority.

Unveiling the Sons and Daughters of God

MONARCH

Romans 8:19 declares, "For the creation waits in eager expectation for the children of God to be revealed." This is the time of unveiling—the time when the true sons of God will be revealed to the world.

This unveiling is not just about identity; it is about authority. The sons of God are those who have been entrusted with His authority to bring Heaven's influence to earth. This unveiling is taking place on multiple levels. First, it is an unveiling of identity and inheritance. Many believers are discovering, perhaps for the first time, who they truly are in Christ. They are realizing that they are not just saved sinners, but they are kings and priests, called to rule and reign with Christ.

Ascension in the spirit is important, growing through from a child to Sonship as an Heir. As we matriculate into Sonship then the Lord entrusts us to advancing The Kingdom of Heaven in the Earth. It begins with ourselves, our family, our community, our nation, our assigned jurisdictions and then generations. We see this as we look at the patriarchs in the Bible such as Abraham and Moses. Galatians 4:1-7

Second, it is an unveiling of purpose. As the sons of God arise, we are being commissioned to fulfill our Kingdom assignments. These assignments are not limited to the church or religious activities but extend into every sphere of society —religion, government, business/economy, education, arts and entertainment, media, and family.

Finally, it is an unveiling of authority. The sons of God are being empowered to exercise Kingdom authority in their respective domains. This authority is not just for the benefit of the Church but for the transformation of the world. As we step into our Kingdom authority, we will see the earth transformed by the power and presence of God.

The Role of Women in This Kingdom Era

In this new Kingdom era, women have a critical role to play. The Lord is raising up women who will walk in their full Kingdom authority, who will lead with wisdom and strength, and who will be catalysts for change in their families, communities, nations and generations. Unlike the feminist movement.

35 – 117

MONARCH

This is not about equality because we were already made equal Genesis 1:26-31; it is about destiny, it is about inheritance. Women are being called to arise as Monarch Woman Kings, to take their place as co-heirs with Christ, and to reign in the authority that has been given to us.

The story of Esther is a powerful example of a woman who walked in her Kingdom authority. When she was called upon to save her people, she did not shrink back in fear but boldly approached the king, knowing that she had been positioned by God for such a time as this (Esther 4:14). Like Esther, women today are being positioned for strategic assignments in the Kingdom. They are being called to intercede, to lead, to influence, and to reign.

This is a time of great empowerment for women in the Body of Christ. The Lord is breaking off the limitations that have been placed upon them, both by society and by the Church. He is restoring their rightful place as co-heirs and co-laborers in the Kingdom. Women are being equipped, anointed, commissioned and sent to carry out the assignments that God has ordained for them, and fulfill their destinies.

Woman King Arise

A Call to Embrace the New Kingdom Era

As we step into this new Kingdom era, there is a call to action—a call to embrace the new, to let go of the old, and to fully step into the authority and identity that God has given us. This is not a time to hold back or to be content with the status quo. It is a time to arise, to take our place as kings and priests unto God, and to advance His Kingdom with boldness and authority.

The Lord is inviting us to partner with Him in this new move of the Spirit. He is looking for those who will say yes to His call, who will align themselves with His purposes, and who will walk in the fullness of their Kingdom authority. This is a time of great opportunity—a time to see the Kingdom of God manifested on earth as it is in Heaven.

The question is, will you answer the call? Will you step into your royal identity and take your place in this new Kingdom era? The time is now. The Kingdom is at hand. Arise, Monarch Woman King, and reign.

37 - 117

Chapter 3: The War for Your Glory

In the spiritual realm, the glory of God on a person represents His presence, favor, and power. It signifies a transformative relationship with God and can manifest as light, holiness, or divine authority. When individuals are filled with God's glory, they reflect His character and bear witness to His greatness, often empowering them for service and demonstrating His love to others.

Notable examples include Moses, whose face shone after encountering God, and Jesus, whose transfiguration revealed His divine glory. However, this glory can become a target for the enemy, who seeks to steal, tarnish, or distort it. This chapter will explore the concept of stolen glory, one of the tactics of the enemy in spiritual warfare that hinder one from rising in Kingdom authority, and how to reclaim and protect the glory that God has given you.

The Concept of Glory: Glory in the biblical sense is not just about radiance or splendor; it is about the weight of God's presence, the honor of His name, and the authority that comes with being His child. Glory is both a gift and a responsibility. It is a reflection of God's nature in you, and it is something the enemy fears and envies. **38 – 117**

MONARCH

How Glory Is Stolen: The enemy targets your glory through lies, trauma, character assassinations, rejection, witchcraft, and spiritual attacks. Just as the enemy tried to strip Jesus of His glory through temptation, false accusations, and crucifixion, he tries to do the same with us. The goal is to undermine your identity, your authority, and your purpose.

- **Lies, character assassinations and Deception**: The enemy uses lies to make you doubt your worth and your calling. He tries to convince you that you are not who God says you are, thereby stealing the glory of your true identity.

- **Rejection, Trauma and Abandonment**: Rejection is a powerful tool of the enemy to make you feel isolated and worthless. This is a direct attack on the glory of being chosen and loved by God.

- **Witchcraft and Manipulation**: Witchcraft, in its various forms, seeks to bend and manipulate outcomes against God's will. It is a direct attack on the glory of God's plans for your life, trying to replace them with counterfeit purposes.

MONARCH

The Battle for Your Glory: The enemy is relentless in his pursuit to sabotage your God-given glory because he understands the immense power of a believer walking fully in their Kingdom identity. When tactics like lies, character assassination, rejection, trauma, and witchcraft fail, he often resorts to using human vessels. These individuals may either be fully aligned with darkness or have left spiritual doors open through which the enemy can gain access—much like a remote control. Through these vessels, the enemy seeks to carry out physical or spiritual assassination attempts, designed to prematurely end a believer's destiny. However, God's divine intervention can intercept and nullify these attacks.

We see this vividly in the life of Samson, who was destined for greatness from birth but fell into the sin trap of Delilah. Delilah, who had aligned herself with the Philistines, became the enemy's instrument to bring about Samson's downfall, by the literal cutting of his hair. Samson's vulnerability, combined with Delilah's manipulation, ultimately led to his capture and blindness.

40 – 117

MONARCH

Samson's hair, which represented his strength and glory, was cut, symbolizing the enemy's attempt to strip him of his God-given authority. Yet, even in his darkest hour, God's mercy enabled Samson to fulfill his final act of destiny (Judges 16:4-30). This serves as a reminder that though the enemy may try to derail our purpose through human agents and devices, God's plan and power always prevail when we return and submit to Him.

Scripture supports this: "The thief does not come except to steal, and to kill, and to destroy. I have come that they may have life, and that they may have it more abundantly" (John 10:10 NKJV). Additionally, 1 Corinthians 11:15 says, "But if a woman has long hair, it is a glory to her; for her hair is given to her for a covering," reinforcing the idea that hair is a representation of glory.

Furthermore, Ephesians 6:12 reminds us, "For we do not wrestle against flesh and blood, but against principalities, against powers, against the rulers of the darkness of this age, against spiritual hosts of wickedness in the heavenly places."

Restoration of Glory

"However, this kind does not go out except by prayer and fasting." Matthew 17:21 (NKJV) This verse speaks to the importance of spiritual disciplines such as prayer and fasting in overcoming particularly challenging spiritual battles, demonstrating that some breakthroughs require deeper commitment and alignment with God's power.

- **Prayer and Fasting:** These are powerful tools to reclaim stolen glory. Prayer aligns you with God's will and releases His power to restore what has been lost. Fasting breaks strongholds and brings spiritual clarity.

- **Read & Pray The Word of God:** Scripture is your sword in spiritual warfare. Declaring God's word with authority is utilizing the Scepter of the Lord. Decreeing over your life silences the lies of the enemy and reaffirms your inheritance, identity and authority.

- **Community and Accountability:** Surround yourself with believers who can stand with you in prayer and provide godly counsel. Isolation is a tactic of the enemy, but unity in the body of Christ brings strength.

42 – 117

Reclaiming and Protecting Your Glory: Reclaiming your stolen glory involves recognizing the enemy's tactics and standing firm in your God-given identity. It is about taking back what the enemy has stolen and guarding it through a close relationship with God.

- **Repentance and Restoration**: If your glory has been stolen due to sin or disobedience, repentance is the first step to restoration. God's grace is sufficient to restore all that has been lost.

- **Daily Armor**: Ephesians 6:10-18 describes the armor of God that protects you in spiritual warfare. Wearing this armor daily ensures that you are equipped to stand against the enemy's schemes.

- **Walking in Authority**: Reclaimed glory must be maintained through walking in the authority God has given you. This means living in obedience, humility, and submission to God's will.

43 - 117

MONARCH

Chapter Conclusion: The battle for your glory is real, but so is the victory that Christ has already won for you. As you engage in spiritual warfare, reclaiming what has been stolen, you will walk in the fullness of your God-given identity and authority. Remember, the glory that God has placed on your life is precious, and it is worth fighting for. Stay encourage for you shall surely recover all that was stolen.

"So David inquired of the Lord, saying, 'Shall I pursue this troop? Shall I overtake them?' And He answered him, 'Pursue, for you shall surely overtake them and without fail recover all.'" 1 Samuel 30:8 (NKJV)

Chapter 4: Dominion Over Witchcraft

Witchcraft is not merely the stuff of fairy tales and folklore; it is a very real and serious threat in the spiritual realm. Throughout history, witchcraft has been used as a tool of the enemy to pervert, manipulate, and control. In this chapter, we will explore the biblical perspective on witchcraft, how it operates, and how, as Kingdom citizens, we have been given authority over all forms of witchcraft. The focus will be on recognizing the subtle and overt manifestations of witchcraft, understanding its dangers, and exercising dominion over it through the power of Christ.

Understanding Witchcraft: Witchcraft is the attempt to manipulate spiritual forces and exert power outside of God's will.

It is rebellion against God, as 1 Samuel 15:23 equates rebellion to the sin of witchcraft. Witchcraft takes many forms—ranging from overt practices like spells and curses to more subtle manipulations like control, domination, and the use of fear to influence others.

- **Biblical Examples of Witchcraft:** The Bible provides numerous examples of witchcraft and its consequences. From Saul consulting the witch of Endor (1 Samuel 28) to the sorcery of Simon the Sorcerer (Acts 8), these stories highlight how witchcraft is an abomination to God and leads to destruction.

- **Modern-Day Manifestations:** Today, witchcraft can manifest in various ways—through new age practices, occult rituals, and even through manipulative behaviors that seek to control or dominate others. It's important to recognize that witchcraft can infiltrate even subtle areas of life, including relationships, institutions, and cultural practices.

The Danger of Witchcraft: Witchcraft is dangerous because it directly opposes God's will and seeks to usurp His authority. It opens doors to demonic influence and can have devastating effects on individuals, families, and communities. The Bible warns against engaging in any form of witchcraft, as it leads to spiritual bondage and separation from God.

46 - 117

- **Spiritual Bondage:** Those who practice or are subjected to witchcraft can find themselves in spiritual bondage, experiencing fear, confusion, oppression, and a lack of peace. This bondage can affect every area of life, including health, relationships, and finances.

- **Separation from God:** Witchcraft creates a barrier between individuals and God, as it involves turning to demonic powers instead of relying on the Holy Spirit. This separation can lead to spiritual dryness, lack of direction, and ultimately, eternal consequences.

Exercising Dominion Over Witchcraft: As Kingdom citizens, we are not powerless against witchcraft. Through the authority of Jesus Christ, we have been given dominion over all the works of the enemy, including witchcraft. This authority must be exercised in faith, using the tools that God has provided.

- **The Name of Jesus:** The name of Jesus is the most powerful weapon against witchcraft. At the name of Jesus, every knee must bow (Philippians 2:10), including the powers of witchcraft.

47 - 117

- When confronted with witchcraft, invoking the name of Jesus brings divine power and authority to the situation.

- **The Blood of Jesus:** The blood of Jesus is a protective covering, evil covenant breaker and a weapon against the enemy. It provides cleansing, protection, and victory over all forms of evil, including witchcraft. Declaring the power of the blood of Jesus over your life, family, and home is a crucial step in maintaining spiritual freedom.

- Using the Blood of Jesus to destroy the works of the devil such as evil covenants. "We have overcome by the Blood of the Lamb and word of our testimony, and they loved not their life unto death". Revelation 12:11 (NKJV). "For this purpose the Son of God was manifested, that He might destroy the works of the devil." 1 John 3:8 (NKJV). "But thus says the Lord: 'Even the captives of the mighty shall be taken away, and the prey of the terrible shall be delivered; for I will contend with him who contends with you, and I will save your children." Isaiah 49:25 (NKJV).

48 - 117

- **The Word of God**: Scripture is the sword of the Spirit (Ephesians 6:17) and is effective in cutting down the lies and attacks of witchcraft. Speaking the Word of God in faith disarms the enemy and reinforces your spiritual authority.

- **Prayer and Fasting**: Prayer, coupled with fasting, is a powerful combination that breaks the strongholds of witchcraft. Fasting humbles the soul and increases spiritual sensitivity, enabling you to hear God more clearly and pray with greater effectiveness.

Examples of Dominion Over Witchcraft:

- **Elijah vs. The Prophets of Baal:** In 1 Kings 18, Elijah confronts the prophets of Baal, demonstrating God's power over the demonic forces they served. His boldness and faith led to a dramatic victory, proving that God's power is supreme over all forms of witchcraft.

- **Paul and the Sorcerer Elymas**: In Acts 13:6-12, the Apostle Paul confronts Elymas the sorcerer, who tried to oppose the gospel. Paul, filled with the Holy Spirit, rebukes Elymas, and the sorcerer is struck blind. This event led to the conversion of many, showing the power of God over witchcraft.

49 - 117

MONARCH

- **Jesus' Ministry**: Throughout His ministry, Jesus cast out demons, healed the sick, and broke the power of witchcraft and sorcery wherever He went. His authority was evident, and He imparted this same authority to His disciples.

Living in Victory Over Witchcraft: To live in victory over witchcraft, it's essential to remain close to God, grounded in His Word seeking understanding by revelation, and submitted to His authority. Regular prayer, worship, and fellowship with other believers provide the spiritual strength needed to resist and overcome any form of witchcraft.

- **Spiritual Discernment**: Ask God for the gift of discernment to recognize witchcraft in all its forms. This will help you identify and deal with it promptly, preventing it from taking root in your life.

- **Spiritual Warfare**: Engage in spiritual warfare through prayer, declaring God's promises found in the word that relates to the attack, and standing firm in your authority in Christ. Remember that the battle is not yours, but the Lord's (2 Chronicles 20:15).

- **Faith in God's Protection**: Trust in God's protection and sovereignty. No weapon formed against you shall prosper (Isaiah 54:17), and God is faithful to protect His children from all harm.

50 – 117

MONARCH

Chapter Conclusion: Dominion over witchcraft is not just a concept; it is a reality for those who are in Christ. As you stand in your Kingdom authority, covered by the blood of Jesus, and armed with the Word of God, you can confidently resist and overcome all forms of witchcraft. Remember, greater is He that is in you than he that is in the world (1 John 4:4). Walk in your authority, exercise your dominion, and live in the victory that Christ has already won for you.

Chapter 5: Kingdom Authority

Authority is granted by God, in the Kingdom, authority is not about domination over humans-- that's witchcraft. It is about serving under the authority of Christ, who has all power & authority in Heaven and on Earth (Matthew 28:18). Power without authority is illegitimate; it is like a soldier wielding a weapon without the backing of a higher command. True Kingdom authority comes from being under God's command, aligned with His will, and carrying out His purposes.

The Foundation of Kingdom Authority:

Kingdom Authority is rooted in submission. To wield Kingdom authority, one must first be submitted to God's authority. This submission is not a sign of weakness but of strength, as it aligns you with the ultimate source of power—God Himself. Jesus, the ultimate example, submitted to the Father's will even unto death, and through this submission, He was exalted and given all authority (Philippians 2:8-11). In James 4:7, we are instructed to "Submit yourselves, then, to God. Resist the devil, and he will flee from you." Submission to God is the key to resisting the enemy and walking in the authority that has been given to us. When we are submitted to God, the enemy has no legal right to operate in our lives, and we can effectively resist his attempts to deceive and oppress us.

MONARCH

Kingdom authority is not something that can be earned or acquired through human means. It is granted by God to those who are submitted to His will and His divine order. Jesus exemplified this perfectly during His earthly ministry. Though He was the Son of God, He chose to submit Himself to the Father's will in all things. In John 5:19, Jesus says, "The Son can do nothing by Himself; He can do only what He sees His Father doing, because whatever the Father does, the Son also does." This submission to the Father's authority was the source of Jesus' own authority. He operated under the Father's direction, and as a result, His words and actions carried the full weight of divine authority. This is the model for all believers—our authority in the Kingdom comes from our submission to God's rule and reign in our lives.

Submission is not about weakness or passivity; it is about recognizing and honoring the authority that God has established. This can be seen in the natural order—just as fish thrive in water and birds in the air, believers flourish when they are in alignment with God's order. When we submit to God's authority, we position ourselves to receive His protection, guidance, and empowerment.

53 - 117

MONARCH

Obedience is the outward expression of a submitted heart. When you obey God's commands, you demonstrate your alignment with His authority. Obedience brings you into the flow of God's power, allowing you to operate in His authority with confidence. Obedience is the natural outflow of submission. It is the act of carrying out God's will as revealed in His Word and through the leading of the Holy Spirit. Obedience is not just about following rules; it is about living in a way that pleases God and advances His Kingdom. The Bible is filled with examples of the blessings that come from obedience. In Deuteronomy 28, God outlines the blessings that will overtake those who diligently obey His commands.

Conversely, disobedience leads to a loss of authority and the consequences of stepping outside of God's protection. Obedience often requires faith, especially when God's instructions challenge our understanding or comfort. Abraham's willingness to sacrifice Isaac is a profound example of obedience that aligned him with God's covenant and established him as the father of many nations (Genesis 22). His obedience was not just an act of compliance; it was a demonstration of his trust in God's promises and His authority.

MONARCH

Humility is the posture that maintains your authority. It is recognizing that all authority comes from God and that you are merely a steward of what He has entrusted to you. Humility protects you from pride and ensures that you remain in a position where God can continue to use you mightily.

Authority is the right to rule, govern, and influence others. It is a legitimate and sanctioned power, granted by a higher authority. In the context of the Kingdom of God, authority is bestowed by God Himself. It is not something that can be seized or taken by force; it must be given. Authority is meant to be exercised in alignment with His will. it is lead with love, wisdom, and responsibility.

Humility is the third pillar of Kingdom authority. In a world that often equates humility with weakness, the Kingdom perspective sees humility as a strength that draws one closer to God. Humility is not about thinking less of oneself; it is about thinking of oneself less and recognizing one's dependence on God. The Bible teaches that humility precedes honor. James 4:10 says, "Humble yourselves in the sight of the Lord, and He shall lift you up." Jesus taught His disciples that the greatest in the Kingdom is the one who serves others with a humble heart (Matthew 23:11-12).

This principle is countercultural, yet it is foundational to Kingdom living. Humility is also a safeguard against pride, which is the downfall of many who have been given authority.

Pride leads to a false sense of security and an inflated view of oneself, which ultimately results in a fall (Proverbs 16:18). Pride is the cause of Satan's found in Isaiah 14:12-15, which describes his desire to ascend above God. In contrast, humility keeps believers in a posture of reliance on God, ensuring that their authority remains legitimate and effective.

Examples of Kingdom Authority in Action:

- **Jesus' Authority over the Storm:** In Matthew 8:23-27, Jesus calms the storm, demonstrating that His authority over nature comes from His submission to the Father. The disciples marveled, asking, "What kind of man is this? Even the winds and the waves obey him!" This authority was rooted in His divine identity and His perfect submission to the Father.

MONARCH

- **The Centurion's Understanding of Authority:** In Matthew 8:5-13, the centurion recognizes Jesus' authority because he, too, is a man under authority. He understands that Jesus only needs to speak the word, and it will be done. This story highlights the relationship between being under authority and exercising authority.

- **Joseph's Rise to Authority**: Joseph's journey from the pit to the palace (Genesis 37-50) is a story of submission to God's process, obedience in adversity, and humility in leadership. Despite the betrayals and hardships, Joseph's authority was established by God and used to save nations.

The Danger of Counterfeit Authority: Worldly power seeks control and often operates through manipulation and fear. In contrast, Kingdom authority is about stewardship and servanthood. The misuse of power, especially in spiritual contexts, leads to what can be described as "Jezebelic" authority—a counterfeit that manipulates and controls. Characterized by deceit, coercion, and a thirst for power. rather than serving and leading. Godly authority, however, empowers others and aligns with God's purposes, bringing life and freedom. The absence of submission, obedience, and humility often leads to the pursuit of counterfeit authority.

57 - 117

This is the kind of authority that seeks to control, manipulate, or dominate others for personal gain. Counterfeit authority is illegitimate and ultimately destructive. It may achieve temporary success, but it lacks the foundation of God's truth and will eventually collapse. True Kingdom authority, on the other hand, is enduring because it is built on the solid foundation of God's principles.

Walking in Kingdom Authority: To walk in Kingdom authority is to walk in alignment with God's will. It requires daily submission, constant obedience, and a heart that remains humble before God. As you embrace these principles, you will find that your authority in the spiritual realm increases, enabling you to fulfill your God-given purpose with confidence and power.

The Bible also provides examples of what happens when individuals operate outside of God's authority. In Acts 19:13-16, the sons of Sceva, Jewish exorcists, attempted to use the name of Jesus to cast out demons. However, they had no real authority because they were not submitted to Christ. The demons recognized this and overpowered them, leaving them beaten and humiliated. This story serves as a warning that power without legitimate authority is not only ineffective but dangerous.

58 – 117

Kingdom of Darkness & Wicked Kings

The enemy understands the power of authority and often seeks to strip believers of their rightful authority in Christ.

This can happen in various ways, such as through sin, disobedience, or deception. When believers step outside of God's will or succumb to the enemy's lies, their authority can be usurped.

In the Garden of Eden, Adam and Eve were given authority to rule over all creation (Genesis 1:28). However, when they disobeyed God and ate from the tree of the knowledge of good and evil, they forfeited their authority to the enemy. Satan, who is described as the "god of this world" (2 Corinthians 4:4), gained a measure of power over the earth because of Adam and Eve's disobedience.

Jesus came to restore what was lost in the Garden. Through His death and resurrection, He disarmed the powers and authorities and made a public spectacle of them, triumphing over them by the cross (Colossians 2:15). He reclaimed the authority and dominion that Adam and Eve lost and has given it back to those who are in Him.

MONARCH

However, the enemy still seeks to undermine this authority by tempting believers to live in ways that are contrary to God's will. He knows that when believers are not submitted to God, they are vulnerable to his attacks and cannot operate in the full authority that has been given to them.

Chapter Conclusion: Kingdom authority is not about wielding power for personal gain; it is about being entrusted with God's power to accomplish His will on Earth. As you understand and embrace this authority, rooted in submission, obedience, and humility, you will find yourself empowered to lead, to serve, and to bring about God's Kingdom on Earth as it is in Heaven.

Chapter 6: Created in His Image—Equal by Design

From the very beginning, God established men and women as equal in value and purpose. Genesis 1:27 states, "So God created man in his own image, in the image of God created he him; male and female created he them." This foundational truth affirms that both men and women are made in the image of God, both carrying His likeness and endowed with His authority.

This equality is not based on human standards or societal norms but on divine design. In the Kingdom, there is no need for women to fight for equality because it has already been granted by God. The real challenge is for women to recognize their identity and authority in Christ and to step boldly into the roles they have been called to fulfill.

Women as Kings and Priests

The Kingdom of God calls all believers, regardless of gender, to function as kings and priests. Revelation 1:6 declares, "And hath made us kings and priests unto God and his Father; to him be glory and dominion for ever and ever. Amen." This royal priesthood is a powerful position of authority, service, and leadership.

61 – 117

MONARCH

For too long, societal structures and religious traditions have limited the roles of women, confining them to certain spheres and excluding them from others. But in the Kingdom, women are called to reign as kings, exercising dominion and authority in every area of life—be it in the family, the marketplace, ministry, or government.

As priests, women are also called to intercede, to stand in the gap, and to minister before the Lord. This priestly role is not secondary or subordinate but is vital to the advancement of the Kingdom of God. Women, like men, are empowered by the Holy Spirit to govern, bring the presence of God into every situation, to offer spiritual sacrifices, and to lead others into a deeper relationship with Christ.

Chapter 7: The Role of Women in the Kingdom

Women have a significant and powerful role in the Kingdom of God. From the very beginning, God created women with a unique purpose and identity, meant to complement and complete His divine plan on earth. This chapter will explore the biblical foundation for the role of women in the Kingdom, highlighting their contributions, authority, and responsibilities. We will also address the challenges women face in stepping into their Kingdom roles and offer encouragement for embracing and fulfilling this divine calling.

Biblical Foundation of Women's Role: The Bible is filled with examples of women who played crucial roles in God's redemptive plan. From the Old Testament to the New Testament, we see women who were leaders, prophets, warriors, and influencers.

- **Created in God's Image:** Women were created in the image of God, just as men were (Genesis 1:27). This means that women carry the divine nature and are endowed with the same spiritual authority and potential to fulfill God's purpose. The equality in creation underscores the value and importance of women in God's Kingdom.

63 – 117

MONARCH

- **Examples of Women in Leadership**: The Bible provides numerous examples of women in leadership roles. Deborah was a judge and prophetess who led Israel to victory (Judges 4-5). Esther, a queen, played a pivotal role in saving her people from destruction (Esther 4:14). In the New Testament, women such as Priscilla, Phoebe, and Lydia were active in ministry and church leadership (Acts 18:26, Romans 16:1-2, Acts 16:14-15).

- **Women as Co-Laborers in Christ**: In the early church, women were recognized as co-laborers in Christ, working alongside men to spread the gospel and build the Kingdom. Paul, in his letters, often mentioned women who were instrumental in the ministry, acknowledging their contributions and leadership.

- **Cultural and Religious Barriers:** Throughout history, cultural and religious barriers have often limited the roles of women, relegating them to secondary positions. These barriers can create feelings of inadequacy or unworthiness, preventing women from fully embracing their Kingdom roles.

- **Spiritual Opposition:** The enemy often targets women with lies and attacks aimed at undermining their identity and authority. This opposition can manifest as fear, doubt, or discouragement, causing women to shrink back from their calling.

64 – 117

MONARCH

- **Balancing Multiple Roles**: Women often juggle multiple roles—wife, mother, career, ministry—making it challenging to prioritize their Kingdom assignment. The demands of everyday life can sometimes feel overwhelming, leading to burnout or a sense of being unqualified.

Encouragement for Women in the Kingdom: Despite these challenges, God has a powerful and unique purpose for every woman in His Kingdom. It's time for women to rise up, embrace their calling, and walk in the fullness of their divine identity.

- **Embrace Your Identity:** Understand and embrace your identity as a daughter of the King. You are loved, valued, and equipped by God to fulfill your Kingdom purpose. Remember that your identity is not defined by the world's standards but by God's Word.

- **Claim Your Authority:** As a woman in the Kingdom, you have been given authority by God to rule and reign with Him. Claim this authority in your life, your family, and your community. Stand firm in the truth of God's Word, and don't allow the enemy to usurp your identity or authority.

65 - 117

MONARCH

- **Support and Empower Other Women:** Part of your Kingdom role is to support and empower other women. Encourage, mentor, and uplift those around you, helping them to discover and walk in their own Kingdom purpose. Together, women can create a powerful force for God's Kingdom.

- **Stay Connected to God:** Your strength and effectiveness come from your relationship with God. Stay connected to Him through prayer, worship, and the study of His Word. Allow the Holy Spirit to guide you, strengthen you, and empower you to fulfill your role in the Kingdom.

Women as Kingdom Warriors: Women are not only nurturers and caregivers but also warriors in the spiritual realm. God has equipped women with unique gifts and strengths that are essential for advancing His Kingdom.

- **The Virtuous Woman:** Proverbs 31 paints a picture of the virtuous woman, who is strong, industrious, capable, and diligent. She is described as one who "girds herself with strength" and "strengthens her arms" (Proverbs 31:17). This strength is not just physical but also spiritual, enabling her to fulfill her God-given roles with excellence.

66 – 117

MONARCH

- **Spiritual Warfare:** Women are called to engage in spiritual warfare, standing in the gap for their families, communities, and nations. The story of Jael, who defeated the enemy commander Sisera, is a powerful example of a woman taking decisive action in a time of war (Judges 4:21). In the same way, women today are called to rise up as warriors, using their spiritual authority to defeat the enemy's plans.

- **Women Kings Arise:** The concept of a Woman King is a powerful one, emphasizing that women are not just support roles but are called to reign and rule in the Kingdom. As daughters of the King, women have the authority to govern, legislate, and bring about Kingdom change in their spheres of influence.

Challenges to Embracing the Role: Despite the biblical affirmation of women's roles in the Kingdom, there are real systemic challenges and obstacles that can hinder women from stepping into their God-given authority.

Chapter Conclusion: Women have a vital and powerful role in the Kingdom of God. From the beginning, God has created and called women to be co-laborers with Him, endowed with authority, strength, and spiritual gifts.

67 - 117

MONARCH

As women rise to embrace their Kingdom roles, they will become key instruments in God's plan to advance His Kingdom on earth.

Don't let the challenges or opposition deter you. Instead, stand firm in your identity and authority as a daughter of the King, and step boldly into the calling that God has placed on your life. The Kingdom needs you to arise and reign as the Woman King you were created to be.

Chapter 8: The Royal Army

The Kingdom of God is not just a spiritual reality but also manifests on earth through the lives and actions of believers. As women kings, you are called to be part of God's Royal Army, a force that operates both in the physical and spiritual realms. This chapter explores the concept of the Royal Army, its structure, the role of women within it, and how to effectively engage in spiritual warfare as part of this divine military force.

Understanding the Royal Army: God's Royal Army is a powerful and strategic force composed of believers committed to advancing the Kingdom of God. Kingdom's take territory, this army operates under the authority of Jesus Christ, the King of Kings, and is equipped with spiritual weapons and armor to defeat the forces of darkness and take territory for the Kingdom of Heaven.

- **Heavenly Army:** The Bible frequently mentions the heavenly hosts, angelic beings who serve God and carry out His commands. These celestial beings are part of the Royal Army, engaged in spiritual battles that impact the earth (2 Kings 6:16-17, Revelation 12:7-9).

- As believers, we are supported by this heavenly army in our spiritual warfare, and we can call upon their assistance through prayer and intercession.

- **Earthly Army**: The earthly aspect of God's Royal Army consists of believers who are called to enforce the Kingdom of God on earth. This involves spreading the gospel, interceding in prayer, standing against injustice, and engaging in spiritual warfare. As part of this army, you are a soldier in God's Kingdom, trained and equipped for battle (Ephesians 6:10-18).

- **Chain of Command**: Just as any army has a chain of command, so does God's Royal Army. Jesus Christ is the supreme commander, and under Him, there are various levels of authority, including spiritual leaders, intercessors, and warriors. Understanding and submitting to this divine order is crucial for effective warfare.

The Role of Women in the Royal Army: Women have always played a vital role in God's army, both in the natural and spiritual realms. Throughout history, women have been warriors, intercessors, and leaders who have advanced the Kingdom of God in powerful ways.

70 – 117

MONARCH

- **Deborah—A Warrior Judge**: Deborah was a prophetess and judge in Israel who led the nation to victory over its enemies. Her story illustrates the strength, wisdom, and courage that women can bring to the battlefield (Judges 4-5). Like Deborah, you are called to be a leader and warrior in God's Royal Army.

- **Esther—A Strategic Intercessor**: Esther's role in saving the Jewish people was not just as a queen but as a strategic intercessor. Through fasting and prayer, she engaged in spiritual warfare that changed the course of history (Esther 4:16). Women in the Kingdom today are called to intercede on behalf of nations, families, and individuals, wielding the power of prayer as a weapon of war.

- **Modern-Day Women Warriors**: In today's world, women continue to play critical roles in advancing the Kingdom. Whether through prayer, leadership, or acts of service, women are at the forefront of the battle, pushing back darkness and establishing God's rule on earth.

Engaging in Spiritual Warfare: As a member of God's Royal Army, you are called to engage in spiritual warfare. This battle is not against flesh and blood but against spiritual forces of evil in the heavenly realms (Ephesians 6:12). Understanding how to fight this battle is essential for fulfilling your role in the Kingdom.

MONARCH

- **The Armor of God**: Ephesians 6:10-18 describes the spiritual armor that every believer must put on to stand against the enemy's schemes. This armor includes the belt of truth, the breastplate of righteousness, the shoes of the gospel of peace, the shield of faith, the helmet of salvation, and the sword of the Spirit. Each piece is vital for protection and offense in the spiritual battle.

- **Weapons of Warfare**: In addition to the armor, God has given us spiritual weapons to fight the enemy. These include prayer, fasting, the Word of God, worship, and the blood of Jesus. When used effectively, these weapons can dismantle strongholds, break chains, and bring about victory in the spiritual realm.

- **Strategy and Tactics**: Just as in any battle, strategy and tactics are crucial in spiritual warfare. This involves listening to the Holy Spirit, discerning the enemy's plans, and following God's instructions carefully. Sometimes this means engaging in intercession, other times it might involve taking action in the natural realm. Being sensitive to God's leading is key to victory.

Royal Family--Victory Through Unity: One of the enemy's greatest tactics is to divide and conquer. In God's Royal Army, unity is essential for victory. When believers come together in prayer, worship, and purpose, they create a powerful force that the enemy cannot withstand.

72 – 117

- The Power of Agreement: Jesus said that where two or three are gathered in His name, He is there in their midst (Matthew 18:20). There is tremendous power in agreement and unity among believers. Whether it's a small group or a large gathering, when we unite in purpose, we strengthen the army of God and advance His Kingdom.

- **Supporting Each Other in Battle:** As part of the Royal Army, it's important to support and encourage one another. This might involve praying for each other, offering words of encouragement, or providing practical assistance. We are not meant to fight alone but as a united force against the enemy.

You Give Your Kings Great Victories: King's are Warriors. The Bible repeatedly emphasizes that kings are not just rulers but also warriors. They are called to lead their people into battle, to defend their kingdoms, and to conquer the enemies of God. This is not just a physical reality but a spiritual one as well. As children of God, and as part of the royal priesthood, we are called to engage in spiritual warfare with the same tenacity and authority that the kings of old demonstrated on the battlefield. Psalm 18:50 declares, "He gives His king great victories; He shows unfailing love to His anointed, to David and to his descendants forever." This verse is a reminder that victory in battle is not just a matter of human strength or strategy but is granted by God to His chosen ones. It speaks of divine favor, anointing, and the assurance that God fights for His kings.

73 - 117

MONARCH

Throughout Scripture, we see this theme of kingship intertwined with warfare:

- David was a king known for his military prowess. From his youth, when he defeated Goliath with just a sling and a stone, to his many battles as king, David's victories were attributed to God's favor and guidance (1 Samuel 17; 2 Samuel 5:19).

- Jehoshaphat, when faced with overwhelming odds, was told by the prophet Jahaziel, "The battle is not yours, but God's" (2 Chronicles 20:15). His victory came through worship and obedience, not through traditional warfare.

- Hezekiah trusted in God when Assyria threatened Jerusalem. Instead of succumbing to fear, he prayed, and God sent an angel to strike down the Assyrian army (2 Kings 19:35).

These examples are not just historical accounts; they serve as spiritual principles for us today. As women called to reign in the Kingdom of God, we are also called to be warriors in the spirit. Our battles may not be with physical swords, but they are no less real. We contend with principalities, powers, and rulers of darkness (Ephesians 6:12). And just as God gave the kings of Israel victory, He promises to give us victory in our spiritual battles.

MONARCH

The Role of the Woman King in Battle: As a Woman King, you are called to stand in the gap, to intercede, and to lead in spiritual warfare. Your authority comes from your identity in Christ and your submission to His rulership. The battles you face—whether in your personal life, your family, your community, or your nation—are not fought with carnal weapons but with divine power.

God equips His kings and queens with the armor of God (Ephesians 6:10-18), the sword of the Spirit, which is the Word of God, and the shield of faith. Your prayers, declarations, and worship are powerful weapons that can bring down strongholds, change atmospheres, and release the Kingdom of God on earth.

Kingdom Victory Through Christ: Victory is not just a future promise; it is a present reality. Through Jesus Christ, we have already been given victory over sin, death, and the powers of darkness (1 Corinthians 15:57).

As you walk in your royal identity and engage in the battles before you, remember that the victory is assured. God has already given you the victory through Christ.

MONARCH

In your battles, whether they are for your family, your community, or even your nation, stand firm in the knowledge that God is with you. He has given you authority as a Woman King, and He will give you great victories as you align yourself with His will and fight in His strength.

Conclusion: As you reflect on the battles you face, remember that you are not alone. The God who gave David, Jehoshaphat, and Hezekiah their victories is the same God who fights for you. You are part of a powerful and divine army that is advancing the Kingdom of God on earth. As a Woman King, your role in this Royal Army is crucial. Whether you are engaging in spiritual warfare, leading others, or interceding in prayer, you are a warrior in God's Kingdom.

Remember that you are not fighting alone—there is a heavenly host backing you, and you are part of a global army of believers committed to seeing God's will done on earth. Stay armored, stay united, and continue to fight the good fight of faith. Victory is assured, for the battle belongs to the Lord. Declare Psalm 18:50 over your life and circumstances and walk in the authority that God has given you as His chosen royal priesthood.

76 – 117

MONARCH

Prayer: "Lord, I thank You that You give Your kings and queens great victories. I declare that in every battle I face, You are with me, fighting for me, and granting me victory. I stand in the authority You have given me as Your royal child, and I trust in Your unfailing love and faithfulness. Just as You gave David, Jehoshaphat, and Hezekiah victory over their enemies, I believe that You will give me victory over every challenge and opposition I face. I put my trust in You, Lord, and I declare that the battle is Yours. In Jesus' name

MONARCH

The Call to Arise

The title "Monarch Woman King Arise" is not just a catchy phrase—it is a prophetic mandate. Women are being called to arise, to wake up to their true identity in Christ, and to take their place in the Kingdom. This call is not about competing with men but about fulfilling the unique purposes that God has designed for women.

Throughout history, God has used women in powerful ways to accomplish His purposes. Deborah, a prophetess and judge in Israel, led her nation to victory (Judges 4-5). Esther, a queen, used her influence and intercession to save her people from destruction (Esther 4:14). Mary, the mother of Jesus, accepted the divine call to bring the Savior into the world (Luke 1:38). These women, and many others, exemplify the courage, faith, and authority that women in the Kingdom are called to demonstrate.

Overcoming Barriers and Breaking Chains

Despite the divine call, many women face significant barriers that prevent them from fully stepping into their Kingdom authority. These barriers include cultural stereotypes, religious traditions, and personal insecurities.

78 - 117

But the time has come for these chains to be broken and destroyed permenantly.

Cultural stereotypes have often confined women to certain roles, suggesting that leadership, authority, and influence are reserved for men. These lies have hindered many women from pursuing their God-given callings. However, in the Kingdom of God, such distinctions are irrelevant. Galatians 3:28 proclaims, "There is neither Jew nor Greek, there is neither bond nor free, there is neither male nor female: for ye are all one in Christ Jesus."

Religious traditions, too, have sometimes limited women, teaching that their primary role is to support rather than lead. While support is important, it is not the only role that women are called to play. Women in the Kingdom are leaders, influencers, and change-makers. They are called to the frontlines of spiritual warfare, to the boardrooms of business, and to the platforms of ministry.

Personal insecurities can also be a significant barrier. Many women struggle with feelings of inadequacy, fear, and doubt. But the Word of God is clear—He has not given us a spirit of fear but of power, love, and a sound mind (2 Timothy 1:7). Women must rise above these insecurities, trusting in God's strength and the authority He has given them.

79 - 117

Empowering the Next Generation

As women arise in their Kingdom authority, they have a crucial role in empowering the next generation. This is not just about mentoring young women but about instilling Kingdom values and principles in both young men and women. The future of the Kingdom depends on this next generation understanding their identity, authority, and purpose in Christ. Hence, the role of women is paramount in the expansion of the Kingdom on Earth.

Women who have gone before must be willing to pour into the lives of others, to share their wisdom, experiences, and insights. This is how the legacy of Kingdom authority is passed down—through intentional discipleship and mentorship. Titus 2:3-5 emphasizes the importance of older women teaching and guiding the younger ones, ensuring that the values of the Kingdom are preserved and advanced.

A United Front—Men and Women Together

And I want women to get in there with the men in humility before God, not primping before a mirror or chasing the latest fashions but doing something beautiful for God and becoming beautiful doing it. I don't let women take over and tell the men what to do. 1 Timothy 2:8-15 The Message (MSG)

While this chapter focuses on the role of women, it is important to note that the Kingdom of God is not divided by gender. Men and women are called to work together, side by side, in advancing the Kingdom. This unity is essential for the Church to operate in its full authority and power.

Men must recognize the value and authority of women in the Kingdom and be willing to support, collaborate with, and empower them. Likewise, women must recognize the importance of unity and partnership with men, understanding that together, they can accomplish far more for the Kingdom than they could apart.

Conclusion: Arise and Reign

The time is now for women to arise and take their place in the Kingdom of God. This is not just a call to action—it is a divine mandate. Women are being called to step into their authority, to break free from the chains that have held them back, and to reign as kings and priests unto God. As women arise, they will not only fulfill their own destinies but will also inspire and empower others to do the same. The Kingdom of God is advancing, and women have a critical role to play in this divine movement. It is time to arise, to embrace your Kingdom authority, and to reign with Christ in every area of life. The next generation of God's Kingdom is awaiting our manifestation.

81 – 117

Chapter 9: Higher levels of Authority

In the Kingdom of God, true authority is not derived from titles, positions, or outward displays of power. Instead, it is rooted in submission, obedience, and humility—three principles that are often misunderstood in the context of leadership and authority. This chapter explores how these qualities are the foundation of Kingdom authority, offering insights into how believers can align themselves with God's order and operate in the authority that flows from His throne.

Aligning with Divine Authority

Submission is often viewed negatively in modern society, where autonomy and independence are highly valued. However, in the Kingdom of God, submission is a powerful principle that aligns believers with divine authority.

Jesus Himself demonstrated submission in His earthly ministry, consistently yielding to the will of the Father, even unto death (Philippians 2:8).

82 – 117

The Centurion's Faith: A Model of Authority

One of the most striking examples of Kingdom authority rooted in submission and humility is the story of the Roman centurion in Matthew 8:5-13. The centurion approached Jesus, asking for the healing of his servant, and expressed his understanding of authority by saying, "For I also am a man under authority, having soldiers under me. And I say to this one, 'Go,' and he goes; and to another, 'Come,' and he comes; and to my servant, 'Do this,' and he does it."

The centurion recognized that Jesus' authority was derived from His submission to the Father. Jesus marveled at the centurion's faith and granted his request, demonstrating that understanding and honoring authority are key to operating in it. The centurion's faith was not just in Jesus' power to heal but in His authority as the Son of God, who is under the authority of the Father.

Enduring Injustice: The Path to Greater Authority

There are times when submission, obedience, and humility lead to suffering or injustice. However, even in these situations, believers are called to endure with grace, trusting that God is in control.

Jesus Himself endured the greatest injustice—the crucifixion—yet His obedience to the Father's will resulted in the ultimate exaltation (Philippians 2:9-11).

In the Kingdom, enduring injustice is often a precursor to promotion. When believers respond to injustice with humility and trust in God, they are positioning themselves for greater authority. This principle is illustrated in the life of Joseph, who, despite being betrayed, falsely accused, and imprisoned, maintained his integrity and humility. In the end, God elevated him to a position of great authority, second only to Pharaoh (Genesis 41:40-44).

Conclusion: Embracing Kingdom Authority

True Kingdom authority is not something to be grasped or wielded for personal gain. It is a divine gift, entrusted to those who submit to God's will, obey His commands, and walk in humility. This authority is powerful because it is rooted in the character of God, not in human strength or ambition.

84 - 117

MONARCH

Believers who embrace submission, obedience, and humility will find themselves operating in a level of authority that transcends earthly power. This authority is what will enable them to fulfill their God-given purpose and to advance His Kingdom on earth as it is in heaven.

85 – 117

Chapter 10: Fulfilling Your Purpose in the Kingdom

Every believer has a unique purpose within the Kingdom of God. This purpose is not just a lofty ideal but a tangible calling and destiny that each of us is meant to fulfill. In this chapter, we will explore the steps to discovering, embracing, and walking in your Kingdom purpose. Understanding your role in the Kingdom is essential to living a life that is both meaningful and impactful, aligning your actions with God's divine plan for your life.

Discovering Your Kingdom Purpose: Your Kingdom purpose is the specific role God has designed for you in His-story, His grand plan. This purpose is intricately tied to your identity in Christ, your spiritual gifts, and your life experiences.

- **Seek God First:** The first step in discovering your Kingdom purpose is to seek God wholeheartedly. Matthew 6:33 reminds us to "seek first the Kingdom of God and His righteousness, and all these things shall be added unto you." In seeking God, you will gain clarity and direction for your life's purpose.

- **Understand Your Spiritual Gifts**: Your spiritual gifts are a significant indicator of your Kingdom purpose. These gifts are given by the Holy Spirit to equip you for the work God has called you to do (1 Corinthians 12:4-11). Take time to identify and develop these gifts, as they will guide you in fulfilling your purpose.

- **Reflect on Your Life Experiences**: God often uses your life experiences, both good and bad, to prepare you for your Kingdom assignment. Reflect on the pivotal moments in your life—times of joy, trials, and breakthroughs—and consider how they have shaped your understanding of God's plan for you.

Embracing Your Kingdom Assignment: Once you have discovered your purpose, the next step is to embrace it with confidence and commitment. Embracing your Kingdom assignment means fully accepting the call of God on your life and being willing to step out in faith, even when the path is uncertain.

87 - 117

- **Overcoming Fear and Doubt:** Fear and doubt are common obstacles to embracing your purpose. Remember that God has not given you a spirit of fear, but of power, love, and a sound mind (2 Timothy 1:7). Trust in God's provision and guidance, knowing that He equips those He calls.

- **Stepping Out in Faith:** Walking in your Kingdom purpose requires faith. Hebrews 11:1 defines faith as the substance of things hoped for, the evidence of things not seen. When God calls you, He will also provide the resources, connections, and opportunities needed to fulfill your purpose. Your job is to step out in obedience, even when you can't see the full picture.

- **Commitment to the Process:** Fulfilling your purpose is a journey, not a destination. It requires ongoing commitment, perseverance, and a willingness to grow and adapt as God leads you. Stay committed to the process, trusting that God is working all things together for your good (Romans 8:28).

Overcoming Challenges in Fulfilling Your Purpose: Fulfilling your Kingdom purpose is not without challenges. Whether it's spiritual opposition, personal struggles, or external circumstances, obstacles will arise. However, with God's help, these challenges can be overcome, and even used to furt effectiveness.

88 - 117

MONARCH

- **Spiritual Warfare:** The enemy will often try to hinder your progress by attacking your identity, your faith, or your circumstances. Ephesians 6:12 reminds us that we wrestle not against flesh and blood, but against principalities and powers. Be vigilant in prayer, put on the full armor of God (Ephesians 6:10-18), and stand firm in the truth of God's Word.

- **Persevering Through Difficulties**: Difficulties and setbacks are a natural part of the journey. Whether it's a personal trial, a delayed promise, or an unexpected challenge, perseverance is key. Remember the words of James 1:2-4, which encourage us to consider it pure joy when we face trials, knowing that the testing of our faith produces perseverance.

- **Staying Focused on the Bigger Picture**: In the midst of challenges, it's important to stay focused on the bigger picture—God's Kingdom and His ultimate plan for your life. Don't get discouraged by temporary setbacks or distractions. Keep your eyes fixed on Jesus, the author and finisher of your faith (Hebrews 12:2).

Fruitfulness and Fulfillment in the Kingdom: When you walk in your Kingdom purpose, your life will bear fruit—both in your own personal growth and in the impact you have on others. This fruitfulness leads to a deep sense of fulfillment, knowing that you are living out God's plan for your life.

- **Bearing Fruit in Every Season:** Psalm 1:3 describes the righteous as trees planted by streams of water, bearing fruit in every season. As you fulfill your Kingdom purpose, you will experience fruitfulness in every area of your life. This fruit may manifest as personal growth, successful endeavors, or the positive impact you have on others.

- **Finding Fulfillment in God's Plan**: True fulfillment comes from knowing that you are living out God's plan for your life. This fulfillment is not dependent on external success or recognition, but on the peace and joy that come from being in the center of God's will. Embrace this fulfillment, and let it be your motivation to continue pursuing your Kingdom purpose.

- **Leaving a Lasting Legacy**: Fulfilling your purpose is not just about your own life; it's about leaving a lasting legacy for future generations. As you walk in your calling, you are paving the way for others to follow, influencing and inspiring those who will come after you. Consider the impact of your life and ministry on your family, your community, and the Kingdom of God.

90 – 117

MONARCH

Chapter Conclusion: Fulfilling your purpose in the Kingdom is one of the most rewarding and significant pursuits you can undertake. It requires seeking God, embracing your calling, and walking in obedience and faith. As you do so, you will experience the joy and fulfillment of knowing that your life is making an eternal impact. Remember, you are called for such a time as this (Esther 4:14), and God has equipped you with everything you need to fulfill your purpose. Step into your calling with confidence, and watch as God uses you to advance His Kingdom on earth.

MONARCH

Chapter 11: Kingdom Commonwealth

In the context of kingship, wealth plays a crucial role in fulfilling the divine purpose of the kingdom on Earth. Understanding this principle is essential for a monarch woman to effectively govern and influence her realm. Wealth, when viewed through the lens of kingdom theology, transcends mere accumulation; it becomes a tool for advancing the agenda of the kingdom and serving humanity.

The Nature of Kingdom Wealth: In the kingdom, wealth is not simply about material possessions or financial resources; it embodies the resources necessary to manifest God's will on Earth. Kingdom wealth includes not only money but also influence, knowledge, and the capacity to create opportunities for others. This holistic view of wealth reflects the nature of God as the ultimate provider, who equips His children to carry out their divine assignments.

Scripture reference, Deuteronomy 8:18 (NKJV): "And you shall remember the Lord your God, for it is He who gives you power to get wealth, that He may establish His covenant which He swore to your fathers, as it is this day."

MONARCH

Wealth as a Resource for Purpose: Every king or queen has a mandate to impact their domain positively. Wealth enables this mandate by providing the means to build, support, and uplift communities. It allows for the establishment of schools, hospitals, and other vital institutions that nurture the well-being of the people. When monarch women recognize their role as stewards of wealth, they can channel resources to fulfill the kingdom's purpose, creating a legacy that aligns with divine principles.

Scripture Reference, 2 Corinthians 9:8 (NKJV): "And God is able to make all grace abound toward you, that you, always having all sufficiency in all things, may have an abundance for every good work." Matthew 25:14-30 (NKJV): The Parable of the Talents emphasizes stewardship and the responsibility to use resources wisely for the kingdom.

The Spiritual Dimension of Wealth: Kingdom wealth is intrinsically linked to spiritual principles. It is rooted in the understanding that all resources come from God and should be used in accordance with His will. This mindset shifts the focus from personal gain to collective benefit. When wealth is approached with a spirit of generosity and stewardship, it becomes a means to bless others and expand the kingdom's reach.

93 - 117

MONARCH

Scripture Reference, Proverbs 10:22 (NKJV): "The blessing of the Lord makes one rich, and He adds no sorrow with it." Luke 16:11 (NKJV): "Therefore if you have not been faithful in the unrighteous mammon, who will commit to your trust the true riches?"

Breaking the Chains of Poverty: In the kingdom, there is no room for poverty when the resources are available to uplift and empower. The church and kingdom leaders must work to break the chains of financial despair by teaching principles of stewardship, investment, and entrepreneurship. A monarch woman can lead the charge in this area, inspiring others to harness their gifts and talents to create wealth that benefits the entire community.

Scripture Reference, Isaiah 61:1 (NKJV): "The Spirit of the Lord God is upon Me, because the Lord has anointed Me to preach good tidings to the poor; He has sent Me to heal the brokenhearted, to proclaim liberty to the captives, and the opening of the prison to those who are bound." Proverbs 21:13 (NKJV): "Whoever shuts his ears to the cry of the poor will also cry himself and not be heard."

94 - 117

MONARCH

The Impact of Wealth on Influence: Wealth brings influence, and influence amplifies the message of the kingdom. When a monarch woman operates from a position of abundance, she can advocate for justice, righteousness, and equity in her realm. Her financial capacity allows her to support initiatives that reflect kingdom values, thus extending her influence beyond her immediate circle. Scripture Reference, Proverbs 22:7 (NKJV): "The rich rules over the poor, and the borrower is servant to the lender." Ecclesiastes 10:19 (NKJV): "A feast is made for laughter, and wine makes merry; but money answers everything."

The Responsibility of Wealth: With the privilege of wealth comes the responsibility to use it wisely. A true monarch woman understands that wealth is not an end in itself but a means to fulfill a greater purpose. This includes being accountable for how resources are acquired and distributed. Ethical stewardship reflects the character of the kingdom and sets an example for others to follow. Scripture Reference, Luke 12:48 (NKJV): "For everyone to whom much is given, from him much will be required; and to whom much has been committed, of him they will ask the more." 1 Timothy 6:17-19 (NKJV): "Command those who are rich in this present age not to be haughty, nor to trust in uncertain riches but in the living God, who gives us richly all things to enjoy."

MONARCH

Conclusion: Arise in Wealth and Purpose, as we explore the relationship between kingship and wealth, it becomes evident that a monarch woman's role is pivotal in demonstrating how kingdom wealth can transform lives and communities. By embracing the principles of kingdom theology, she can rise to her calling, utilizing her resources not only for personal enrichment but as a powerful force for good in the world. In this journey, let us remember that wealth is a vehicle for purpose. As monarch women arise in their roles, they have the unique opportunity to redefine wealth in their communities, ensuring that it serves the greater good and reflects the heart of the kingdom.

With this understanding, the call to leadership becomes a call to empower others, heralding a new era of abundance and purpose in the kingdom. Scripture Reference, Philippians 4:19 (NKJV): "And my God shall supply all your needs according to His riches in glory by Christ Jesus." Matthew 6:33 (NKJV): "But seek first the kingdom of God and His righteousness, and all these things shall be added to you."

Chapter 12: Expressions of the Kingdom of God

The Kingdom of God is not just a spiritual concept; it is a reality that is meant to be expressed and manifested in every aspect of life. As women kings, you are called to bring the Kingdom of God into every sphere you influence—whether in your home, workplace, community, or nation. This chapter explores how the Kingdom of God can be expressed through your life and how you can become a conduit of God's presence, power, and purpose in the world.

Understanding the Kingdom of God: The Kingdom of God is the rule and reign of God over all creation. It is the fulfillment of God's will and purposes on earth as it is in heaven (Matthew 6:10). The Kingdom is both a present reality and a future hope, and it is expressed through the lives of those who submit to God's authority and live according to His principles.

- **The Nature of the Kingdom:** The Kingdom of God is characterized by righteousness, peace, and joy in the Holy Spirit (Romans 14:17).

97 - 117

MONARCH

- It is a Kingdom where justice prevails, mercy is extended, and love is the foundation. As believers, we are called to embody these characteristics in our daily lives.

- **Kingdom Mindset**: To express the Kingdom of God, you must first adopt a Kingdom mindset. This involves seeing the world through God's eyes, understanding His priorities, and aligning your thoughts, actions, and desires with His will. A Kingdom mindset is focused on eternity, values humility over pride, and seeks to serve rather than be served.

Manifesting the Kingdom in Your Life: The Kingdom of God is not limited to the four walls of the church; it is meant to permeate every area of your life. As a woman king, you have the privilege and responsibility of manifesting the Kingdom in your personal life, relationships, work, and community.

- **In Your Personal Life:** Your personal relationship with God is the foundation of your ability to express the Kingdom. Through prayer, worship, and studying the Word, you align yourself with God's will and allow His Kingdom to be established in your heart. Personal holiness, integrity, and obedience are also crucial in manifesting the Kingdom in your life.

- **In Your Relationships**: The Kingdom of God is a Kingdom of love. As you interact with others—whether in your family, friendships, or community—you have the opportunity to express God's love, grace, and forgiveness. Healthy, God-centered relationships are a powerful testimony of the Kingdom.

- **In Your Work**: Whatever your vocation, you are called to do your work as unto the Lord (Colossians 3:23). This means striving for excellence, maintaining integrity, and being a light in your workplace. Whether you are in business, education, healthcare, or any other field, you can bring the Kingdom of God into your work environment by being a godly influence and demonstrating Kingdom principles in your actions.

- **In Your Community:** As a representative of the Kingdom of God, you are called to impact your community for Christ. This might involve participating in local outreach, advocating for justice, serving the needy, or simply being a positive presence in your neighborhood. By living out the values of the Kingdom—such as love, compassion, and humility—you can make a tangible difference in your community and bring others closer to God.

Expressions of the Kingdom Through Ministry: Ministry is a key way through which the Kingdom of God is expressed. Whether you are called to full-time ministry or ministering in your daily life, you have a unique role in advancing the Kingdom.

- **Preaching and Teaching**: Sharing the Word of God is one of the most direct ways to express the Kingdom. Whether through formal preaching, teaching, or personal conversations, you can help others understand and embrace the Kingdom of God. It's important to be grounded in scripture and led by the Holy Spirit to effectively communicate the truths of the Kingdom.

- **Intercession**: Prayer is a powerful tool for bringing the Kingdom of God to Earth. Through intercession, you can pray for God's will to be done in specific situations, regions, and lives. This not only aligns you with God's purposes but also releases His power to effect change in the world.

- **Service and Acts of Kindness**: Jesus said that whatever we do for the least of these, we do for Him (Matthew 25:40). Serving others, whether through practical acts of kindness or more organized efforts, is a direct expression of the Kingdom. It demonstrates God's love and care for all people, especially the marginalized and oppressed.

100 – 117

MONARCH

The Role of Creativity in Expressing the Kingdom: Creativity is a powerful and often overlooked way to express the Kingdom of God. God is the ultimate Creator, and as His children, we are called to reflect His creativity in our lives and work.

- **Creative Arts**: Music, art, dance, writing, and other forms of creative expression can powerfully communicate the values and truths of the Kingdom. These forms of art can inspire, encourage, and lead others to a deeper understanding of God. Whether you are a professional artist or simply enjoy creative activities, your work can be an offering to God and a tool for Kingdom advancement.

- **Innovation in the Marketplace**: Creativity is not limited to the arts. Innovative ideas and solutions in business, technology, and other industries can also reflect the Kingdom of God. As a woman king, you can bring Kingdom values into the marketplace by developing products, services, and business models that honor God and serve people.

Living as a Kingdom Ambassador: As a citizen of the Kingdom of God, you are also an ambassador, representing the King in every area of life. This is both a privilege and a responsibility.

MONARCH

- **Ambassadors of Christ:** 2 Corinthians 5:20 says that we are Christ's ambassadors, imploring others to be reconciled to God. As an ambassador, your life should reflect the values, priorities, and character of the Kingdom. This means living with integrity, showing love and compassion, and boldly sharing the gospel.

- **Cultural Influence:** The Kingdom of God is meant to influence culture, not just exist alongside it. As an ambassador, you have the opportunity to shape culture in ways that align with God's will. This might involve challenging societal norms that are contrary to Kingdom values, promoting justice and righteousness, and creating spaces where the Kingdom of God can be experienced by others.

Chapter Conclusion: The Kingdom of God is vast, encompassing every aspect of life and eternity. As a woman king, you are called to be an active participant in expressing and advancing this Kingdom. Whether through your personal life, relationships, work, ministry, or creativity, you have the opportunity to make the invisible Kingdom visible in the world around you. By living as a Kingdom ambassador, you can bring hope, healing, and transformation to a world in desperate need of God's love and truth. Embrace your royal identity and step into your role as a vessel of God's Kingdom on earth.

102 - 117

Chapter 13: Living out Your Royal Call Practically

In the spiritual realm, our royal identity is not just a symbolic gesture but a fundamental reality rooted in biblical truth. Ephesians 2:6 declares, "And raised us up with Him and seated us with Him in the heavenly places in Christ Jesus." This passage affirms that we are elevated beyond the earthly realm, seated with Christ in heavenly places, which underscores our exalted status and divine authority. 1 Peter 2:9 further illuminates our identity: "But you are a chosen race, a royal priesthood, a holy nation, a people for His own possession, that you may proclaim the excellencies of Him who called you out of darkness into His marvelous light." This verse signifies that our royal status is inherent to our identity as believers, chosen and set apart to declare God's glory. Revelation 5:10 also reinforces this concept: "And have made us kings and priests to our God; And we shall reign on the earth." This promise highlights our role not just as subjects, but as co-rulers with Christ, participating in His divine authority and reign.

Royal Calling Practical

Embracing our royal identity involves more than understanding it intellectually; it requires living it out in our daily lives.

103 – 117

MONARCH

This realization transforms our perspective and behavior. As Women Kings, we are called to reflect the majesty of our divine heritage through our actions, choices, and interactions.

1. Upholding Righteousness

Our royal calling necessitates living a life of righteousness. Psalm 45:6-7 describes the King as one who loves righteousness and hates wickedness. As royal heirs, we are to embody these values, aligning our lives with God's standards and demonstrating integrity in every aspect of our existence.

2. Exercising Kingdom Authority

With our royal identity comes divine authority. Luke 10:19 assures us, "Behold, I have given you authority to tread on serpents and scorpions, and over all the power of the enemy, and nothing shall hurt you." This authority enables us to overcome challenges and influence our surroundings in accordance with God's will.

3. Impacting the World

Our Kingdom status empowers us to make a positive impact on the world. Matthew 5:14-16 likens believers to a city set on a hill and a light shining before others.

104 – 117

MONARCH

This metaphor emphasizes our role in illuminating the truth and advancing God's Kingdom in every sphere of influence we inhabit.

The Practical Application of Kingdom

Understanding and embracing our royal identity has practical implications. It influences how we approach our roles, relationships, and responsibilities. By living out our divine calling, we honor our position as heirs to the Kingdom and fulfill the purpose for which we have been created.

1. Personal Transformation

Embracing our royal identity leads to personal transformation. Romans 12:2 encourages us, "Do not be conformed to this world, but be transformed by the renewal of your mind." As we align our thoughts and actions with our royal calling, we experience spiritual growth and renewed purpose.

2. Influence and Leadership

Our royal identity positions us as leaders in various capacities. 1 Timothy 2:1-2 urges us to pray for those in authority so that we may live peaceful and godly lives. This call to prayer and intercession reflects our role in guiding and influencing others through divine wisdom.

MONARCH

Conclusion

The call to royalty is a profound and transformative journey. As we embrace our identity as Women Kings, we step into our divine purpose and wield the authority bestowed upon us by God. This chapter lays the foundation for understanding how to cultivate and live out this royal calling, setting the stage for the subsequent chapters that will further explore the dimensions of our spiritual inheritance.

MONARCH

Kingdom Prayers

Chapter 1: Embracing Your Royal Identity Prayer/Declaration:

"Father, I thank You that I am fearfully and wonderfully made in Your image. I declare that I am a royal priesthood, a chosen generation, called to show forth Your praises. I embrace my identity as a King and Priest unto You, and I walk in the fullness of my authority in Christ. I renounce every lie of the enemy that seeks to diminish my worth or question my identity. I am who You say I am, and I stand firm in that truth. In Jesus' name, Amen."

Scriptural Backing: 1 Peter 2:9, Psalm 139:14, Revelation 1:6

Chapter 2: Identifying Your Spiritual Gifts Prayer/Declaration:

"Lord, I thank You for the unique gifts and talents You have placed within me. I ask for Your wisdom and guidance in identifying and cultivating these gifts for Your glory. I declare that I will not bury my talents but will use them to advance Your Kingdom.

I ask that You would stir up the gifts within me and help me to operate in them with boldness and confidence. May I serve others with a heart of love and humility, knowing that every good and perfect gift comes from You. In Jesus' name, Amen."

Scriptural Backing: 2 Timothy 1:6, James 1:17, 1 Corinthians 12:4-7

Chapter 3: Walking in Your Anointing as a Woman King Prayer/Declaration:

"Father, I thank You for the anointing that You have placed upon my life. I declare that I will walk in my anointing with boldness, humility, and authority. I will not be intimidated by the enemy, but I will stand firm in the power of the Holy Spirit. I ask that You continue to fill me with Your Spirit and empower me to fulfill the calling You have placed on my life. May I be a vessel of honor, used for Your glory, and may Your anointing break every yoke of bondage. In Jesus' name, Amen."

Scriptural Backing: Isaiah 61:1, 1 John 2:20, Zechariah 4:6

Chapter 4: Understanding and Embracing Kingdom Authority Prayer/Declaration:

"Lord, I thank You for the authority that You have given me as a child of God. I declare that I will walk in Kingdom authority, understanding that greater is He that is in me than he that is in the world. I renounce every attempt of the enemy to strip me of my authority, and I stand firm in the power of Your Word. I submit to Your rulership, knowing that in submission to You, I am equipped to rule and reign. May I exercise this authority with love, wisdom, and discernment. In Jesus' name, Amen.

" Scriptural Backing: Luke 10:19, 1 John 4:4, James 4:7

Chapter 5: The Spiritual Battle for Your Royal Identity Prayer/Declaration:

"Father, I thank You for revealing the battle that rages for my identity in Christ. I declare that I will stand firm in the truth of who I am, wearing the full armor of God to withstand the attacks of the enemy. I reject every lie, every accusation, and every attempt to steal, kill, or destroy my identity.

MONARCH

I declare that I am victorious in Christ and that my identity is secure in Him. No weapon formed against me shall prosper, and every tongue that rises against me in judgment I shall condemn. In Jesus' name, Amen."

Scriptural Backing: Ephesians 6:10-18, Isaiah 54:17, John 10:10

Chapter 6: Stolen Glory and Spiritual Warfare Prayer/Declaration:

"Lord, I thank You for restoring my glory and my honor. I declare that every area of my life where the enemy has sought to steal, kill, or destroy is being restored sevenfold. I take back what was stolen from me, and I declare that I will walk in the fullness of my destiny. I bind every spirit of witchcraft, every curse, and every form of spiritual attack against my life, and I release the blessings, favor, and protection of God over me. I declare that my glory is being restored, and I will shine forth Your light for all to see. In Jesus' name, Amen."

Scriptural Backing: Joel 2:25, Proverbs 6:31, Isaiah 60:1-2

110 – 117

Chapter 7: Dominion Over Witchcraft Prayer/Declaration:

"Father, I thank You for the authority You have given me over all the power of the enemy, including witchcraft. I declare that no weapon of witchcraft formed against me shall prosper. I break every curse, hex, spell, and incantation spoken against me in the name of Jesus. I declare that I am covered by the blood of Jesus, and the forces of darkness have no power over me. I command every assignment of the enemy to be canceled and every stronghold to be broken. I stand in my authority as a Kingdom ambassador, and I declare victory in every area of my life. In Jesus' name, Amen."

Scriptural Backing: Luke 10:19, Galatians 3:13, Isaiah 54:17

Chapter 8: Fulfilling Your Purpose in the Kingdom Prayer/Declaration:

"Lord, I thank You for the purpose and calling You have placed on my life. I declare that I will fulfill my purpose with passion, diligence, and faithfulness. I ask for Your guidance and wisdom to navigate the path You have set before me. I renounce every spirit of fear, doubt, and confusion, and I choose to walk by faith and not by sight.

111 - 117

MONARCH

I declare that every gift, talent, and anointing You have given me will be used for Your glory and the advancement of Your Kingdom. I commit my plans to You, trusting that You will establish my steps. In Jesus' name, Amen."

Scriptural Backing: Jeremiah 29:11, Proverbs 16:3, 2 Timothy 4:7

Chapter 9: The Role of Women in the Kingdom Prayer/Declaration:

"Father, I thank You for the unique and powerful role that women play in Your Kingdom. I declare that I will rise up as a Woman King, embracing my authority and my calling. I will not be silenced, intimidated, or held back by societal norms or expectations.

I declare that I am a daughter of the Most High, and I will fulfill my role with grace, strength, and courage. May I be a light in the darkness, a voice for the voiceless, and a vessel of Your love and power. In Jesus' name, Amen."

Scriptural Backing: Esther 4:14, Proverbs 31:25-26, Galatians 3:28

Chapter 10: The Royal Army: Earthly and Heavenly Prayer/Declaration:

Woman King Arise

MONARCH

"Lord, I thank You for enlisting me in Your royal army. I declare that I will fight the good fight of faith, knowing that I am not alone but surrounded by a great cloud of witnesses and backed by the heavenly host. I will stand firm in the face of adversity, knowing that the battle is not mine but Yours. I declare that I am more than a conqueror through Christ who loves me. I ask for divine strategies and supernatural strength to fulfill my mission in Your Kingdom. May I always be aligned with Your will and Your purposes. In Jesus' name, Amen."

Scriptural Backing: 2 Timothy 2:3-4, Romans 8:37, 2 Chronicles 20:15

Chapter 11: Expressions of the Kingdom of God Prayer/Declaration:

"Father, I thank You for the diverse and beautiful expressions of Your Kingdom on earth. I declare that I will be a true reflection of Your Kingdom, manifesting Your love, justice, peace, and righteousness in all I do. I will be a conduit of Your grace, a messenger of Your truth, and a vessel of Your power. I ask that You continue to reveal to me the ways in which I can express Your Kingdom in my life, my community, and the world. May Your Kingdom come, and Your will be done on earth as it is in Heaven. In Jesus' name, Amen."

Scriptural Backing: Matthew 6:10, Romans 14:17, 2 Corinthians 5:20

MONARCH

Source Citation

Biblical References

• Holy Bible, King James Version (KJV). Cambridge Edition: 1769. Public Domain.

• New International Version (NIV). © 1973, 1978, 1984, 2011 by Biblica, Inc.

• English Standard Version (ESV). © 2001 by Crossway Bibles, a publishing ministry of Good News Publishers.

Books and Commentaries

• Munroe, Myles. The Purpose and Power of Authority: Discovering the Power of Your Personal Domain. Destiny Image, 1997. Referenced for teachings on Kingdom authority, submission, and personal dominion.

• Munroe, Myles. Understanding the Purpose and Power of Prayer: Earthly License for Heavenly Interference. Whitaker House, 2002. Referenced for insights on the authority given to believers in prayer and operating under God's divine order.

MONARCH

• Bevere, John. Under Cover: The Promise of Protection Under His Authority. Thomas Nelson, 2001. Referenced for principles on submission, authority, and spiritual protection.

• Prince, Derek. They Shall Expel Demons: What You Need to Know About Demons – Your Invisible Enemies. Chosen Books, 1998. Referenced for discussions on spiritual warfare and the power of Kingdom authority over demonic forces.

• Wagner, C. Peter. Spiritual Warfare Strategy: Confronting Spiritual Powers. Destiny Image, 1996. Referenced for understanding spiritual warfare and the role of Kingdom authority in confronting witchcraft and demonic powers.

Pamela I. Emmanuel's Works

• Emmanuel, Pamela I. A King's Prayer. AKingsPrayer.com, 2021. Referenced for Kingdom-focused prayer strategies and intercession for divine authority and governance.

• Emmanuel, Pamela I. A Queen's Prayer. AKingsPrayer.com, 2021. Referenced for teachings on the role of women in the Kingdom, emphasizing their authority, intercession, and spiritual impact.

115 – 117

MONARCH

Articles and Online Resources

• Meyer, Joyce. "Understanding Humility and Confidence in God's Will." Joyce Meyer Ministries. Accessed [Date]. www.joycemeyer.org. Referenced for the discussions about humility, confidence in God's will, and avoiding false humility.

Additional References

• Matthew 28:18 (KJV): "And Jesus came and spake unto them, saying, All power is given unto me in heaven and in earth." Referenced in the discussion on Kingdom authority granted by Jesus.

• Psalm 118:22 (KJV): "The stone which the builders refused is become the head stone of the corner." Referenced in the section on promotion and spiritual authority through enduring rejection.

• Luke 9:1 (KJV): "Then he called his twelve disciples together, and gave them power and authority over all devils, and to cure diseases." Referenced in the discussion of power and authority granted by Jesus to His disciples.

116 – 117

Woman King Arise

MONARCH

CROWNED COLLECTION COLORING BOOKS

& MORE
AKINGSPRAYER.COM

Woman King Arise

www.ingramcontent.com/pod-product-compliance
Lightning Source LLC
Chambersburg PA
CBHW020938160726
48196CB00101B/773/J